Katie is an autistic and physically disabled writer who creates performance poetry and interdisciplinary poetic storytelling for theatre. They write complicated metaphors about serious things, like sickness, loss, and love. Their writing is highly political, with a queercrip and cripplepunk ethos, aiming to tell challenging and subversive stories that destabilise the nondisabled norm.

In 2014, Katie was a winner of the SLAMbassadors youth slam, and they've stuck to the stage ever since. They have performed at festivals including Greenbelt and Shambala, and worked on commissions for Homotopia and Theatre Absolute. In 2019, they co-founded the disability arts organisation Radical Body, where they produce radical new performances by and for disabled people.

My Body is a Resource I am Willing to Expend

(poems of sickness, loss and love)

Katie (Tom) Walters

Burning Eye

BurningEyeBooks
Never Knowingly
Mainstream

Copyright © 2022 Katie (Tom) Walters

The author asserts the moral right under the Copyright, Designs and Patents Act 1988 to be identified as the author of this work.

All rights reserved. No part of this publication may be reproduced, stored in a retrieval system, or transmitted, in any form or by any means without the prior written consent of the author, nor be otherwise circulated in any form of binding or cover other than that in which it is published and without a similar condition being imposed on the subsequent purchaser.

This edition published by Burning Eye Books 2022

www.burningeye.co.uk

@burningeyebooks

Burning Eye Books
15 West Hill, Portishead, BS20 6LG

ISBN 978-1-913958-22-0

For Ruth Spink,
For telling me I was wrong when I was wrong
And for telling me I was right when I thought I was wrong

Content warnings: this collection includes mentions of suicide, mental illness, eating disorders, physical illness, death of a loved one, medical abuse and eugenics.

(But I like to think that, with all this in mind,
the collection is broadly a happy one.)

Contents

Clinically Vulnerable	10
The Elevator Is Out of Service; Please Use the Stairs	12
Air Hunger	15
The Sumatriptan Blues	16
Why I still cry whenever someone offers me a tangerine	18
For Peter, who never knew me	19
Elegy for the Rat King	21
Song of the jinbei-zame	22
My body is a resource I am willing to expend	24
Can I mourn for things I never had?	26
The Words I Have Not Spoken	27
The day I learned that turning eighteen doesn't mean it's sensible to drink	30
Keep me burning	32
Struwwelkatie	35
Fuck you if your legs work	36
Resuscitate Me!	39
Carcinise with Me	44
Gospel of Big Fat Love	45
In Captain Corelli's Mandolin…	48
My boyfriend lives in bed	50
For Julia, in Spring	52
Run and Fly	53
Waking up at 3pm on a Tuesday and no longer feeling embarrassed about it	54

One evening I came home
To find you'd turned into a tree
And shed your dressing gown for bark.
I brought you tea.

I poured it to the floor
So you could drink it with your feet
And sat beneath you at the table,
Asked you how your day had been.

I listened to your silence
And gave you all my bones
To fertilise the carpet
Of our decomposing home.

You rooted in the roof
Of the flat beneath our own
And grew up through the ceiling
Of our living room.

Upstairs, I found your boughs
In the U-bend of our sink,
In the wiring of our bedroom
And in the printer ink.

I pulled out all my fingernails
And planted them like seeds,
Tore up all my skin into
The blossom for your leaves.

And I lay back on our mattress
And waited 'til I grew.
In all the places you had been
I bloomed into your fruit.

Clinically Vulnerable

The question of whether or not I am still a person
Is one that rings in my head on the regular.
If I am a person, I've decided that only I am allowed to ask it.
To my doctor I say *fuck you, I am human*.
Even if I don't feel it much.
The whole world has shut down from this virus
And, if I'm honest, I wouldn't have
Noticed if I didn't go on Twitter.

I don't know why I keep going on Twitter
When the nausea is more of me than me is.
And I'm so thirsty for sleep,
Like that cough that made me so thirsty all the time
That I couldn't stop drinking
When my stomach got heavy and full with the water
But my throat still felt dry.
I'm sleeping like the pint glass I gasped for at 3am
That I didn't need and needed so badly
That drinking it hurt.

> And I wonder if I am sleeping for all the doctors and nurses,
> and the bin men and supermarket workers and the truckers
> and cleaners and the carers who change the catheters of old
> ladies and don't have enough hand sanitiser.

In a dream I go to the sleep bank,
Sit in a wipe-clean sterilised seat,
Where the night-shift phlebotomist
Slips her needle under my eyelid,
Sharp-scratch!
And bleeds out my sleep.
Can I stick that on the list of achievements
On my hospital passport?

Poet
Husband
Daughter
Sleep-donor
Please resuscitate

I only know what day it is because my pill box tells me.
(This is a secret I must keep from the triage nurse.)
If I do not take my meds then there's no evidence of today.
I wonder if this way
I could live forever.
If I never take them again,
Could I make tonight into the world's longest Thursday?
Could I make this one night last as long as a good long life?

The Elevator Is Out of Service; Please Use the Stairs

I
Chronic fatigue took my bones when I was sleeping.
Crept in while I was resting,
Breathing deep against my pillow,
Between the pages of the books I could no longer read.
It grew inside me,
Drank my mitochondria like wine,
Took an angle grinder to my spine
And wore me away like twilight.

I got sick at uni,
On the floor of my kitchen where my legs were burning
Like the oven door against my forearms
And the stovetop, where I made myself curry. For the first time.
Independence, embryonic.
I was nineteen.

November was cold that year, and
January was colder.
As fresh and new as I was, and as
Stark and clean and painful as my fading autonomy.
I tried to crystallise it
In an essay, or a poem, in biro ink and off-brand toothpaste,
Like if I wrote it right I could write myself well,
And when the rain fell in February
I fell. In Tesco and at the train station and on the stairs.
Swallowed the stones in my throat,
Chose not to dare question
Why it was that I kept falling
And got back up.

Because strong people don't get sick.
You stick it out, you do not quit,
And when the elevator is out of service,
You use the stairs.
I never knew how high the kerb was until I could not climb it.

II

We searched for my bones in decomposing diagnoses,
Degrading medication on my tongue,
Took blood tests of my blood lines
And on the coastline
Tried to calcify my insides strong again.
Put our hands in the wet sand
To build a tibia. Shape my sternum like a castle.
Clavicle and mandible and cranium.
Starlight and seafoam and gone.
My bones are in the Rotunda Museum,
Under the skin of the Gristhorpe man.
We walk where he walked, and I walk no longer.
I am pressed behind glass, my skin tight as leather.
My bones are in the limestone cliffs' edge,
Grown from sediment,
Calcium carbonate, cycling, infinite, ground down to shale.
My bones are food for minke whales.

And I am lying in bed, and ugly, like a princess.
Limp, and formless, and rolled out to sea.
I am blue badge on double yellows,
Pepsi Max and heavy metal,
Flat on the back seat,
Looking through the windscreen,
Where the starlings will dance until nightfall.

My bones are a murmur of starlings,
Dark and undulating,
The shapeless shape of nature,
Inexplicable,
Impermanent
And strong.
And I will not be another fucking tragedy,
Another DWP dispensability.
Too many of us have already died.
We build on their bodies. Defiant.
I am a being of duty and fury,

And I want you to know that I am broken
Because they could not contain me whole.

Chronic fatigue took my bones, and they grew.
Fragmented, transcendent and new,
I am fragile. And grounded.
Bound by dropped kerbs and sick insides.

But my bones?

Oh, my bones are the sky.

Air Hunger

I am lying awake in bed and it feels like I am dying.
My husband is fast asleep at my side.
There is no one to bear witness to this suffering.

I am following the instructions from the nurse.
I breathe in for seven seconds and breathe out for eleven,
But my body still believes that I am suffocating.

The doctor does not think this is a problem,
Because no matter how I feel I am not actually suffocating.
I just have hungry lungs.

Since this will not kill me, I am supposed to stay hungry.
Until you die, after all, starvation is a diet.
So I've been told that it's best to keep gasping for sleep

And rearrange my furniture to try and build a life
That I can fit inside the peak
Of one strong breath.

The Sumatriptan Blues

Slowly I've been watching you disappear.

I remember the space that you used to take up.
We've known each other long enough for me to know
The shape of you Before
(At least a little).
There's the echo of you on my skin.
Like a bruise, I feel the absence only when I touch it
Roughly, with a curious hand, sick to know if the hurt is still there.
(Of course the hurt is always still there.)

There is a fire in your brainstem. Both of us can hear it burning.
It has eaten through collagen and now it is pressing
Brain fluid into your optic nerves, it is pressing
Earbuds in, in the waiting room
Your tinnitus is a smoke alarm, but the doctors,
They keep telling you to clear your head and breathe in deeper.

Slowly I've been disappearing too.

I can't get a lumbar puncture.
Two years now with no relief and the painkillers taste like curses,
The co-codamol tastes like the blunt edge of a promise.
I can't open NHS envelopes.
The fear makes my hands shake, and I lie in the dark
While my neighbour applauds out the window.
Somehow we are still alive
And I don't know if I should call that a miracle or a
Crime.

I think we should go to the ocean.
The air is good.
You can breathe it even when you're sleeping
And it won't leave the taste of a hospital floor in your throat.
I think we should live like soft-bodied things.
Shed our spines and become new invertebrates.
Love like cuttlefish

This is how I dream.
But awake I take blood tests until my blood vessels collapse and ask again to be referred to neurology and you are emptying your savings account at an MRI machine with no safety net because under austerity this is the cost of
Hope.

Why I still cry whenever someone offers me a tangerine

When they called the ambulance, I told them not to tell my mother.

They told her anyway.
She walked all the way to sixth form
In her big winter coat.

I was lying on the floor,
Carefully shaped into the recovery position,
Still conscious
But desperate for sleep.
I remember how the fibres of the carpet tile pressed into my face
And how I told them to let me pass out.

I thought she would be angry. But she was nothing.
In the hospital she sat by the bed
And gave me a satsuma.

She peeled it in the shape of an elephant.
The way she had when I was young.
I asked her to leave the room
When they did my psychological assessment.

They drew a curtain so no one could see me,
Left her in the corridor,
Holding questions in her chest
And a fistful of orange peel.

For Peter, who never knew me

I bought plants, with the money you sent me.
Ugly ones.
With no flowers, and with sprawling tendrils.
I built a garden on my windowsill.
It was a generous gift

It didn't take long for you to die, after you sent it.
On a concrete-grey Monday in autumn.
I knew before I answered the phone
What my dad was going to say,
Like I felt it in my heart, or something?
Like I saw it on the bus. From the priority seats.
Or in the leaves of the tradescantia plant
Unfurling itself tenderly by my window.
Trembling, I sensed it.
You died as suddenly
As green leaves grow brittle.

If we hadn't had a funeral, I don't think I would
Have noticed that you were gone.
Sometimes I still don't; I still have dreams about you.
Where you're not dead yet,
And you *did* become a footballer!
At eighty-two, and with fucked-up knees.

You aged into a tree,
Curling, carbonising.
Limbs solidifying into
bark. Liver spotted like moss.
You swayed in the wind,
And your heart hardened too.
Arteries twisting like roots.
And the first we knew,
You'd stopped beating.

You were so loved.
And so *ignorant*. So selfish and kind.
I said goodbye to you in silence.
I couldn't speak for all the secrets held beneath my tongue.

You never met my first girlfriend.
You never knew my real name.

But I will bring your walking stick to my wedding.
So that I can still be holding your hand.
(The hardwood's not that different from the rigid diabetic
 palms you died with.)

I'm gonna plant you on my windowsill.
I will grow you.
I'm gonna whisper my secrets to your leaves when they open.
I'm going to build you a monument
From the suitcase you never gave up on,
Held together by duct tape and faith.
We will fill it with pot plants.
Sprawling and thirsty ones
That are hard to keep alive.
That keep asking.
That curl in summer, and I will coax back to life for the
 greenest autumns.

Elegy for the Rat King

In memory of Tai, 1996–2017.

The night you died,
The city vermin stirred.
Naked tails twitched in the dark
And shining black eyes turned to stare at the moon.
Tiny dark hands reached out to offer you
Stale bread. Discarded fruit.
Anything worthless and sweet.
The eyeless street cats
Took stock of their crippled bodies,
Chose not to harass
Gout-twisted pigeons and injured rats.
Just for the night.

And the fat mother possum
Who lived beneath your porch,
Fur heavy with birth,
Ran out to the park
To tremble in the grass
And teach her children of loss.

Song of the jinbei-zame

The Kaiyukan Aquarium in Osaka, Japan, keeps a whale shark. In 2010, I am lucky enough to visit. My spotty blue vest top matches the spots on its big blue back. Twelve years old, I already believe I'm too big.

The fish on the walls of my bedroom are glow-in-the-dark.

For the rest of my life I will have nightmares about killing my pet goldfish.

In my dreams, I forget to feed him for weeks or months.

When I wake up I don't know. I really don't know if that's how it happened.

Whale sharks are the biggest fish in the world. The largest specimen on record was eighteen metres long. They have cartilage instead of bones, and unlike most sharks they don't have any teeth.

My fish book is an A to Z. A dictionary of fish. It's not an encyclopaedia, but to me it might as well be, because that book is my whole world. I know fish facts like Bible verses. We watch Blue Planet and I recite David Attenborough's lines before he says them.

At the time, I'm unaware that this is a symptom of a diagnosable condition.

It's a filter feeder, the whale shark. The same is true of basking sharks, which are the second biggest fish, though it's a close-run thing. Both enormous filter feeders, they're completely unlike other sharks.

What most people imagine when they picture a shark is something with teeth.

What I imagine when I picture a shark is nothing at all.

It's called aphantasia, common amongst people with autism spectrum disorder.

They're the only extant species of the family Rhincodontidae. And basking sharks are the last of Cetorhinidae. There is nothing else like them on Earth. Strange relics of a different type of life.

I'm fifteen, and a clinical psychologist tells my parents that there's no cure for being like me. I'm in the room and I stare at my shoes.

In 2010, I let go of Dad's hand, and I slip through the crowd to see the whale shark. I press my nose against the glass and watch her eat. Nine metres long and impossibly perfect, she has never even heard of teeth.

My body is a resource I am willing to expend

If she is a temple,
Her stones are wearing under footfall,
And I am still letting in tourists to stare at her statues.
If she is a forest,
I am building a quarry amongst her trees.
Environmentalists have been protesting the exploitation for months now.
I am causing irreparable soil erosion
In my own small intestines.

I'm on stage when I feel the crack in my ribcage
Of an ancient redwood collapsing inside me.
The deforestation is taking hold, now.
I swallow the sound without flinching.
My ecosystem is capable of adapting
To anything.

I have not missed a single work engagement.
Industry is good for the economy, after all,
And I believe the rainforest might recover,
So I devastate her.
I ride the bus to business meetings,
Spread carpet tile over the leaf litter
And climb the stairs at a hundred bars for open-mic nights.
I believe that I am doing a good job.
My occupational therapist tells me that I need to stop.

I am becoming increasingly envious of trees.
Of how they can photosynthesise sunlight into glucose.
Of how sunlight is free.
And how nobody asks them to do anything.
I am pulling up my roots every morning and heaving them into a wheelchair.

At night time, I wrap my body in the softest blankets.

And she begs me to please stop using her like this.
Nothing in nature is infinite.

I tell her, *One day all this will be over.*
One day I'll take you back home.
But I can't do that yet.
I'm not ready.

She will ask again tomorrow.
I will continue to use her up.
But right now, she is soft, and warm, and loved.

I tell her that my pot plants are hardy.
You can sever their stems and strip off their leaves,
But if you put them in soil,
They will grow.
And one day, I hope
To find the courage to plant her.

I tell myself, soon. We'll do it soon.

Can I mourn for things I never had?

I wonder if one day I will be able to accept
That the plans we've been making,
They're probably not going to happen.
They keep piling up.
I've been collecting them tenderly.
The picnics, the foods I am planning to bring you,
The dessert I am planning to invent.
I have been filing them away
Somewhere inside myself
I think I am still intending to bring you everything.
Like one day you'll open your front door to discover
Everything I've ever texted you a photo of.
And I will have brought you Canada.
A moose will lay down its great head on your porch,
And the nodosaur fossil they found in Alberta,
Perfect stone eyelids
On its perfect stone eyes.
I'll bring it to you.
This is no less impossible than being with you on your birthday.
I know exactly how I want your cake to look.
I keep it in my chest,
In the hole torn out when I realised
I would never be an astronaut.
I think I will spend my whole life holding space for you.
Making plans that we cling to like a talisman.
Next time. Next time.
Next time we're going to see the minke whales.

The Words I Have Not Spoken

I don't know how I fit into this house anymore.
All white and crooked, like a tooth, and ageless.
But my elbows hit the walls in ways they didn't use to.
I curl on the piano stool like a curse.
And knock the coats off the coatrack
When I brush through to the kitchen.
It's as if I got taller somehow.
But I didn't.
I don't know how you fit in here either.
I haven't seen you here in a while.
It's like somewhere along the line we
Made new homes,
And changed our shapes.

Our house was the white one. You couldn't miss it.
Detached in a road full of terraces,
Old as bones and illogical.
With floorboards shifting under the skin
Of the carpet.
And a well beneath the lino of our kitchen.
When you were born, our mother chipped you out of
    plasterboard.
Dad laid you down in a blanket to soak up your dust.
You slept a lot, at first.
It takes time, after all, to bring a building to life.
But once you'd opened your eyes,
They shaped me from the stuffing of a mattress.

We grew up sticky.
The way kids are sticky
With jam and sap, soil and grapefruit juice,
Sticky with life.
With the smell of rain,
The smell of tiny moss forests,
Welly boots and grimy hands,

Smells that sit in the back of your nose until you can taste them.
So small. And so loved.
But somehow getting bigger made us feel like not enough?

You started reading those Cathy Glass books.
Books about all the terrible things that have happened to children.
You fell in love with your headphones.
And I don't know when the fear crept in;
I just know that it grew.
The way bathwater grows cold
When you have been playing for too long.

The saddest thing
Was seeing how small you became.
Shrinking into doorways, and bookcases,
And the space beneath your bed.
You had this
Special secret sickness.
It tasted like cereal bars,
Got up far too early
And had friends who didn't trust me,
Who didn't know about the pizza I made you on Wednesdays,
Or how we ate oven chips while they were still frozen.
Or the stories spoken over the melted cheese that was my love for you.

How long were you subsiding on dust?
How many days did I watch you drag your bed
To school on your back?
While the crack of your heart
Ached as taut as a drumskin,
You fought like a tree,
Desperate to grow
And with so little chance of survival.
You had so little chance of survival.

When I look at photographs sometimes I wonder where we went.
I don't know how to comprehend the distance between now and then.
We were children. And now we're this?
Too big for the living room.

I can't find us in this house anymore.
Your tiny aching body,
Or the place where they pulled you from the wall.
And my bedroom is so much smaller
With all the bed scooped out.

And what a privilege it is to knock our elbows against the doorframes of our bedrooms,
To burst through the roof and the windows,
To grow like bamboo, to
Propagate like mycelium.
What a miracle it is that you did not die here.

I saw you so small on the floor of the kitchen.
I saw you silent and shrinking to the size of a fingernail.
I saw your ribs peeking out of
Your vertebrae bursting through your skin.

I saw you stand up from your bed,
Pull your steel toecaps so tight against your feet,
Bust down the front door of our house and walk away.
I see you running, running, running.

The day I learned that turning eighteen doesn't mean it's sensible to drink

It's 2016. I'm eighteen.
I might be an adult, but I'm definitely not a proper grown-up yet.
It's my friend Nathan's eighteenth birthday party, and I am *drunk*.
My girlfriend went home early. Said she felt sick.
I know something's up, but she doesn't wanna talk, so I drink.

I'm lying with my head in the lap of a boy who I quite like really.
Even though I don't like boys.
He runs his hands through my hair, and he says something no boy has ever said to me before, until today.
He tells me that I'm beautiful.
He tells me, Don't you ever cut your hair.

I think maybe he's gonna kiss me, but he
Never does, and that's a good thing, really.
When I leave the party, it's, like, 5am. Everybody's sleeping.
I'm meant to stay over, but I can't close my eyes.
I just don't feel safe.

I walk home.
Don't tell anyone that I'm going, though I know that I should,
And nobody texts me to check where I went. If I got home safe.
I *do* get home safe, but that's still gonna sting in the morning.

I wrap myself in a blanket and tread softly in the dark,
Remember that my sister made this pilgrimage once before.
Barefoot, took herself home all the way from Canley.
When she did it I thought she was mad, but I get it now.

Sometimes you get knots in your stomach that you can only untangle at home.
In a single bed that you've outgrown,
Stargazing at polystyrene ceiling tiles,
Realising that even alone you still feel too big.

And the problem wasn't just that you were at a party, but that
you were *you* at a party.

I get home just in time to switch off my alarm clock.
Curl up on our sofa and make myself tiny.
The cat arranges himself lazily by my side.
Soft as anything, this small creature trusts me not to destroy him,
Though I easily could, if I tried.
That's what I'm thinking about when I decide.

When I tell the story later I will claim that I was drunk,
But the truth is I was stone-cold sober
When my mum shaved my hair off.

She says, *I'll do it, but you're cleaning up the mess.*

Keep me burning

She sits in the church,
Perched on the edge of a wooden pew,
Rests her feet on stone,
Feels her body heat start to
Leach out through the thin soles of formal shoes that were always too slim for her.

A tapestry adorns the walls,
And she's pretty sure you're not supposed to draw God,
Wonders: is this not a false idol, at the head of their
Worship?
Eyes unfeeling and unseeing as
She believes her god to be.
She's not sure when she became so disgustingly unholy.

She doesn't know when it started,
When the seeds were planted,
But they rooted and they grew, and now
She's got lilies in her heart
And there are lilies in the altar vase and,
Glassy-eyed, she stares past the pastor,
And the psalms can't reach her
Anymore.
She is numb.

She has been numb for some time.
Stifled,
Like the sunbeams, and silence,
Or the stained glass eyes
Of an empty cathedral.

She has been curling at night
Around a hollow inside herself,
Feeling extinguished
As the drowned paschal candle.
She hung herself up

And with a spear in her side
She let them cut her shame out.

She thought she'd be lighter without it,
But she is lightless.
She's no longer frightened, but *God* she is hopeless,
And faithless,
And fuelless.

And he tells her she will burn?
So unworthy that her decaying empty is somehow still
    flammable?
He will still burn something so sodden,
In fear of women, and the things that women do in the dark.

The lilies in the vase, they are severed,
They are drowning and
Oh.
She *is* burning.
Rage swelling in her chest,
Red-eyed white-hot fire in her insides.
Oh, and if God lives, then he is dead to her,
Because he certainly doesn't deserve her.
He doesn't deserve her thrumming heartbeat,
Or the flushing cheeks of the girl she has been seeing
When she closes her eyes and she dreams.
The pastor cracked open the stone door of her tomb,
And now, oh, how she is resurrected!
Glory borne out of something spectral, decrepit.
She has had enough, today.
She is Icarus.
She will fly to the sun, and fuck him if he burns her,
And fuck him if he drowns her.
She is going to be glorious,
No matter what the cost.

She sits, in the church,
Perched on the edge of a wooden pew, but she is not cold
    anymore.

She is defiant, she is heroic.

Yes, she thinks, yes,
I am burning.

Struwwelkatie

They call me scruffy Katie.
I'm shaving off my hair.
If people don't like how I look,
I simply do not care.

I will not shave my armpits;
I'll only shave my head.
My clothes will not be beautiful
But comfortable instead.

My face might not be ugly,
But I hope it will be soon.
I want to be a wizened crone,
My only friend the moon.

I'll walk into the forest,
No shoes upon my feet.
I'll feel the mud between my toes
And live amongst the trees.

Leaves will be my pillow,
And moss will be my bed.
I'll drink the moon instead of wine,
And soil will be my bread.

Some folks will think I'm crazy,
And probably they're right,
But I will dance beneath the stars
And sing into the night.

They call me scruffy Katie.
However people tease,
They will not make me grow my hair,
For I do as I please.

Fuck you if your legs work

I'm starting a gang.
We're getting jackets.
Tearing holes in our denim
And sewing on patches,
Stickers on our wheelchairs and crutches in pastel.
I dare you to call me a cripple.
These bitches are
Hardcore.

My girls got blood tests on the regular,
Daily injections
Combating infections,
Neglected by defective immune systems.
My boys got steroid shots,
Nerve pain shooting like lightning bolts
Through their leg braces
And neuralgic faces, at night.
We are ready for a fight.

See, we've been
Breathing in nails, for a while now.
Been living in pain, for a while now.
We got joints cracking
Like baseball bats
In our arthritic hips,
Subluxing numb fingertips,
Our bloodied lips,
Bloodied noses
And throats.
We got blood in our stomachs
I bet you wouldn't dare to digest yourself.

Cripples like me, we got power
When you won't make eye contact, don't know how to deal.
Don't know how to feel about my wheelchair,
That's power.

That sick-stomach sinking shrinking feeling, when I ask if there's
     a place that I can piss in this building, and there *isn't*.
That's power.
Your awkward ass can't not look stares.
I eat that shit for breakfast.

So call me a spastic,
Sick body, retard,
Hard luck, pity fuck,
Call me a broken body,
Ugly body, wrong body,
Should've been a dead body.
I am unapologetically a cripple.
I am not scared of your
Abled body,
Hateful body
Sticking to my crippled body.
Rather have a sick body
Than an ignorant body.

Bring me your cripples.
Ugly cripples, fat cripples,
Misshapen and broken and bitter cripples,
You are my sisters. And brothers.
Siblings and friends.
I will care for you.

Together, we're gonna
Make all our outsides as strong as our insides.
Gonna put on steel toe caps
And leather jackets.
Spikes on our spoke guards,
Brass knuckles on our wrist supports.
Gonna make ourselves hard as the world is.
Not gonna suffer in sick-silence, no.

I'm starting a gang.
We aren't scared of the night.
We've got needles for bones,

And we've got life. Real life.
Screaming and kicking and vital life,
Blue lights and white knuckles, fighting for life,
Doing and being and sick of your shit.
So when we talk you better listen.
'Cause there ain't ever been *nothing* more punk than a cripple.

Resuscitate Me!

A Homotopia Festival commission.

I

These days I only go out at night.
I breathe in deep, to feel the cold air sharp in my chest,
Fear twitching in my fingertips.
Shake off the stress, and I run.
I run the way you only can with wheels.
When I close my fists I wrap my knuckles in my wrist braces.
My palm heels reinforced with steel.
Head down, shoulders back. Downhill.
For a moment I am weightless. I am infinite.

At the crest of the hill a fox flashes across the road.
Bright orange and bold, she is vermin.
I am legally obliged to kill her if I catch her.
Humanely, of course.
She is searching for food.
Tracing the echo of the woods that used to grow here,
She is a bandy-legged wily survivor,
Ready to tear apart bin bags to satiate her hunger.

These days when I run there's something behind me –
Shapeless and smelling of formaldehyde.
I don't know what I fear more, the plague or the doctors,
But the trick is to never let them catch you.
Bite whenever someone touches you.
Snarl whenever they get near.
Hackles up and ugly.

II

When I sleep, I dream of being old.
White-haired and wizened,
My face grown as ancient as my bones.
My clinical frailty score disqualifies me from ICU admission
And I am only twenty-two years old.
On the news they say not to panic,
The people at risk have underlying conditions,
And what I hear is that people like me aren't worth panicking for.
I promise you that death is not an underlying condition.

Nobody says it out loud, but everyone knows
That when doctors choose who to save
They also choose who to not save.
This is uncontroversial for as long as *you* remain saveable.
The newspapers will describe these as tough decisions,
Decisions nobody should ever have to make
That we are making anyway.
And it scares me that all of the dead look the same.
They call this pragmatics,
But I see eugenics.

When you live as a cripple you learn to breathe in death.
The line between living and dying is blurred
'Cause both living and dying are verbs
And you can't do the first without
barrelling
towards
the second.

If it's always at your back, then why not wear it?
Like a leather jacket, like your torn-up jeans,
Like a middle finger.
Why not bear every scar as your armour
With our backhands bruised by cannulas?
Tangled in cheap white bedsheets,
I have tasted concrete on the backs of my teeth.
What we know now is nothing other than

What we have always known.
This is the curse we carry under our fingernails.
It is the truth that we keep clenched in our fists.
That our worth is less
And our breath reminds you of your death,
And our bodies are a barely spoken threat.
We know our place; it is impossible to forget.

We have always been the lives that
You keep hidden in the dark.
We've been forced into poverty
For the sake of austerity,
Forced out of our houses and
Warehoused in care homes,
Dying of sepsis, from neglected infections.
We've been sick and scared and uncared for
For a hell of a lot longer than this.
The only difference now is that it's harder to deny.
That people have stopped feeling embarrassed about it
And started asking us to fill out DNRs.

III

I will tell you right now that I am not going to beg for my life.
This is not an appeal for sympathy;
This is a battle cry.
My words are not for you.
They are white-knuckled fury and life.
Punching and screaming.

Everything we have has come from blood.
From anger and pride,
From dying messy and ugly
And crawling tooth and nail up the steps of the capitol building.
Asking nicely doesn't get you shit.
If I am vermin, I will wear that label for as long as it remains true.
I will not flinch from it.

I will reserve my worth for people who don't ask for it.
I will keep my softness for my crippled siblings.
We will toughen up our outsides to keep our insides gentle.
When they can't breathe, I will be their lungs.
I will dig my fingers under my skin,
Draw blood to lend my strength to them.

IV

Life will move on, but I will remember
The chests of my brethren,
Torn out to free up ventilators.
Whose breath was fed to
Bodies less ugly and flawed and
Beautiful.

And I will call this injustice
Because fuck their consensus.
Because medical ethics aren't written by cripples.
And my ethics don't accept preventable deaths as inevitable.
We are just as worthy of life.

Ventilate us.
In all of our fucked-up glory.
All our misshapen, muscle-wasted, migraine-heavy glory
With our subluxing hips, misfiring synapses, snapping tendons,
Ventilate us.
Unemployed and undesirable, bread line benefit dependents.
Ventilate us invalids, unfortunates and dissidents,
Teeth gritting, sharp-tongued, survivors.
Let us fight; we have been fighting our whole lives.

Pity won't save lives, but fury might.
I will tear open bin bags with my teeth to feed my family.
And will make myself so ugly that people can't stand to look at me,
Hackles up, let them look at me anyway.

I will bite whenever someone touches me,
Snarl whenever they get near.
And if they catch me
I will die loudly. Die publicly, die ugly.
Die humanely, of course.

Carcinise with Me

Carcinisation is the process by which
Evolution converges on the crab.
Because the body of the crab is
Perfect. More Perfect than mine.

We carcinise.
I embrace this with the certainty of Birth.
Inevitable as time.

Hold my hand as we become
small creatures.
Brittle and delicious, and
Clothe ourselves in calcium.
Hold my hand as we begin a new pilgrimage to the sea.

Gospel of Big Fat Love

The world is so heavy,
It would have you believe that you are its weightiest burden.

The floorboards creak beneath your feet.
Under heavy blanket nighttime silences,
Your footsteps crack loud as a gunshot.

You stop dead.

      Deep breath.

Try to tread lighter than your body will let you.
In your own home you move like an intruder,
Bated breath across the landing,
Hoping nobody will notice all the oxygen you steal while they are sleeping.

When no one is awake,
If you feel brave, you thought,
You might stop holding your stomach in.
But with your mother's words ringing in your head
Stark as an early morning car alarm
Those two extra inches of you are a threshold
You're not ready to cross,
And with good reason.

We know that your mother *does* love you.
But you are an expert at slipping into gaps you shouldn't fit through,
At pressing yourself between the cushions of your sofa,
And how are you supposed to live here knowing
That she might love you more if you
Changed?

You avoid eye contact with the mirror when you brush your teeth.
I pretend not to notice you thinking
Of how *proud* she is watching your sister make herself vanish.

Tonight you will sleep with the windows open,
Hoping the cold could be what finally works you to the bone.
I watch you wrap yourself up in another layer of skin,
Tenderly trying to shrink.
Knowing you're probably not going to shrink.
Having to live with knowing that still you kept trying to shrink.

How many times have we questioned if living like this makes us sinners?

Every moment of my body is a crime, every cell oversize,
And the stretch marks on your thighs
Are the warning on a cigarette packet.
We are well above your daily guideline allowance of sodium.

Let me tell you a story I've never told anyone.
Let me find every inch of yourself you've been trying to hide.
Let me witness you.

Let me make every inch of you known.
Let me make it all loved.

How many scales have seen the soles of your feet?
How many plugholes saw your tonsils,
How many doctors saw your body and tried to get you to tear off a piece?
Don't give them anything. Don't give an inch.
Let me tell you you don't have to change, let me tell you to stay
like
this.

Girl, you are a soft and feathered thing.
You are as precious as a cloud.

How could any part of you be wrong?
How could anybody want you less?

Do you really think that sin could be this beautiful?
Do you think I drink in sin when these fingertips touch your skin?
Did we braid it into your ponytail,
Did we spill it over your carpet,
Taint the photos on your bedroom door, or—
Are we *perfect*?

The two of us know the taste of cold water like an old friend.

And I know that in the morning you will swallow it down again, but not tonight.

Tonight I love you like the full moon.
My ocean swings to your gravity,
I dance to the song of your body and,
Until the sun rises in the morning,
I can love us like this.

In Captain Corelli's Mandolin…

There's this story about two trees
Who grow into one,
And I wanted to believe
That was a good thing.

Slowly,
We have been corresponding
With short letters
That I don't know how to pronounce.
I've been sending you pictures
That I mean as words.
Or words that I mean as
A great and nameless feeling that I don't know how to-

-gether,
We've been cultivating seedlings
In our teeth.
Small green things
That taste
Of something
New.

Their roots
Have grown into my molars.
They are finding my nerves and I think that's a good thing.
We are finding them oxygen.
Catching enough of the same breaths.

I can never catch enough breath.
Perhaps I should send you a blanket
That could hold us when we are heavy.

When I am heavier than the tracks of all the trains to the north,
And you are heavier than the concrete of the roads,
And the both of us are heavier than our phones.

Slowly
I've been putting out branches
That only you can see.
Sprawled across the ceiling of my bedroom.

Slowly, I've been growing new root systems.
Winding through the stuffing of my mattress,
Reaching towards the groundwater.

Pictures that I mean as words,
And words that I mean as a feeling,
And roots that we have grown from the same mother seed,
Reaching for each other
Through the bottom of our beds.

When you smile,
I smile.
In a different room.

My boyfriend lives in bed

A poem from my partner's perspective.

My boyfriend lives in bed.
He is there when I leave him in the mornings,
And most days,
He is still there when I come back home again.
I am accustomed to leaning down for a hug, now.
I lie beside him to say goodbye;
He lifts up his arms to welcome me home.
If he's awake.
With the lights down, I sit with him,
And wish that I could lift his pain away.

He doesn't have a kitchen, in his bed.
I make him tea in my kitchen.
I live in a home with more rooms than it has duvets.
I hope he'll move back into them, someday.
Until then, I make tea.

My boyfriend is a sunbeam, muted by blankets.
However often we change the pillowcases,
His head remains framed by a halo of sweat stains.
He burns. And he shines.
He's got a star caught inside him. It drinks in his heartbeats.
He sleeps so he can feed it.
When he opens his mouth, it slips out and it hangs in the air.
It keeps my fingers warm.

We keep the curtains drawn.
Because some days, the sun is too sad.
Because the branches beyond the glass are laughing at him.
Because he loves to climb trees.
I catch him when he falls on the way to the bathroom.
I watch him when he showers, in case he slips, and I bring him a towel that I wrap him in.

He apologises.

And I sigh, 'cause he says sorry a lot,
And it makes me sick inside sometimes,
Like there's something that he wants me to be angry for.
Like he thinks he's not enough.
Like all of this life is just work, and not love.

My boyfriend is a sunbeam, drowning in blankets.
But he is still shining.
At night time, I slip under the covers beside him,
And read a book by his light.

When he wakes up, I will hold him.
He will write me a lullaby with his fingertips.
Bridge the distances of time, and sleep, and silence.
I will wrap him up warm, and carry him out
To see the trees beyond his window.
Press his fingers to the grass.
And we will look at the same moon.
I will hold him as if he were tiny
And I will tell him that I love him big.

For Julia, in Spring

Before spring, the bluebells curl in the soil,
A tight kernel of life, a communion of frozen earth.

In the garden, small green things slip through the cracks,
Gasps of air between paving slabs.

We pick up the shrapnel; a surgical job,
Fine tweezers in trembling hands.

Clear dirt from the rock.
Leave space for the moss.

The lawn, stiff with frost,
Comes warm beneath our footfall.

We breathe deep.
Fill our lungs with birth.

When cold sunbeams pierce the morning air.
When the great open sky calls out
A promise from an old friend.

Hearts thick with loss, we remain,
We become,
We rejoice.

Run and Fly

My extra-extra-large dungarees
Have got sunflowers on.
They are bright blue and bursting with yellow!
I wear my joy across extra-extra-large skin, and,
Rich with seeds, I turn my face towards the sun.

Waking up at 3pm on a Tuesday and no longer feeling embarrassed about it

Today, I spent my whole day being radiantly still.
Being crippled under the covers,
And growing from my mattress
(Like a promise).
Today I spent my day coughing up shame
Like it were curses. Fervently purging it,
Reclaiming my worth.

Today,
I was not productive.
Today I refused to produce.
I did not contribute, and I did that on purpose.
Tucked my self-respect into the hems of my blanket, instead.

Today I spent my whole day doing radical nothings,
Mourning for the body I had lost.
I told her that I loved her.
And I told her she is gone.
I cannot contain her in the person I've become.

She's not welcome here anymore.
I will chase the dust of her from my brainstem,
the promise of her from my lungs.
I told her there will be no home for her to come back to.
That I cannot live in this body with all her stuff still here.

Today I had my breakfast without her.
I sat at the table alone.
I sang myself a little song of stillness,
And I asked absolutely nothing of my bones.

Acknowledgements

Great thanks to Bridget, for taking the time to make my words much better than they would have otherwise been. Editors are magic.

To Ruth, Fen, Manatee, and my wonderful husband Jamie; there are poems in this book for each of you. I hope they go some small way to expressing how profoundly I love you.

To Elle, for understanding me, witnessing me, and pushing me forward when I would have stood still.

To Ace, my ride or die, for your lifelong and unwavering faith in me.

To Hannah Barker, Jess Green, Joelle Taylor, Roger Robinson, Steve Dearden, Stevie Ronnie, Gonzalo Garcia. Ruth Spink, Poppy, Mum, and Dad. This book is the result of a lifetime of support from the best teachers anyone could have asked for.

To Cameron Lauder, who has indirectly touched my life in profoundly influential ways.

Most of all, thanks to my crip siblings. I love you all. Stay tender, strong, and brilliant.

Lightning Source UK Ltd.
Milton Keynes UK
UKHW041354240522
403452UK00013B/269